WELCOME TO MY COUNTRY

Welcome to
HUNGARY

FRANKLIN WATTS
LONDON•SYDNEY

This edition first published in 2006 by
Franklin Watts
338 Euston Road
London NW1 3BH

This edition is published for sale only in the United Kingdom and Eire.

© Marshall Cavendish International (Asia) Pte Ltd 2006
Originated and designed by Times Editions–Marshall Cavendish
An imprint of Marshall Cavendish International (Asia) Pte Ltd
1 New Industrial Road, Singapore 536196

Written by: Chang Shuh Cheng & Nicole Lundrigan
Designer: Rachel Chen
Picture researchers: Thomas Khoo & Joshua Ang

A CIP catalogue record for this book
is available from the British Library.

ISBN-10: 0 7496 7020 7
ISBN-13: 978 0 7496 7020 7

Printed in Malaysia

Franklin Watts is a division of Hachette Children's Books.

PICTURE CREDITS
AFP: 36
alt.TYPE/Reuters: 38
Archive Photos: 15 (all)
Bes Stock: cover
Sue Cunningham: 10 (top), 17, 18 (bottom),
   19, 24, 27, 32
Focus Team Photo Agency: 1, 3 (top), 3 (bottom),
   6, 7 (both), 16 (top) 22, 23, 26, 35, 40,
   41 (top)
Getty Images/HultonArchive: 11, 12 (bottom),
   29, 31
Bridget Gubbins: 21
Blaine Harrington: 16 (bottom), 41 (bottom)
The Hutchison Library: 34
MTI (Hungarian News Agency): 20, 39
Photolibrary.com: 8, 25, 30, 45
Topham Picturepoint: 2, 3 (centre), 4, 9 (both),
   10 (bottom), 12 (top), 13, 14, 18 (top), 28,
   33, 37
Top Foto: 5

Digital Scanning by Superskill Graphics Pte Ltd

Contents

Words that appear in the glossary are printed in **bold** the first time they occur in the text.

Welcome to Hungary!

Because of its central location on the continent, Hungary is often called the "crossroads of Europe". The country was established when Magyar **tribes** crossed the Carpathian Mountains, in about 896, and settled along the Danube River. Let's find out more about Hungary's history and culture.

Opposite: Although it looks like a fortress from the Middle Ages, Fisherman's Bastion in Budapest was built between 1895 and 1902.

Below: Vajdahunyad Castle in Budapest is one of Hungary's most magnificent historical buildings.

The Flag of Hungary

The colours of Hungary's flag represent strength (red), faith (white) and hope (green). This flag was introduced between 1848 and 1849, during a rebellion against the ruling Hapsburg Empire of Austria.

The Land

Hungary has an area of 93,030 square kilometres. It is a **landlocked** country, with Slovakia and Ukraine to the north, Romania to the east, Serbia and Croatia to the south, and Slovenia and Austria to the west. Budapest has been the country's capital since 1873. It is the largest city in Hungary and was formed by uniting the three older cities of Buda, Óbuda and Pest.

Below:
The Danube River divides Budapest into the hilly Buda area to the west and the flatlands of Pest to the east.

The Hungarian Plains

Most of Hungary is flat plains. An **arc** of hills, volcanic peaks and **plateaus**, extending from the Bakony Mountains to the Northern Mountains, divides it into the Little Hungarian Plain and the Great Hungarian Plain. The Little Hungarian Plain, or Little Alföld, is northwest of the arc, while the Great Hungarian Plain, or Great Alföld, is southeast. Mount Kékes is the highest peak, at 1,014 metres.

Above: *Csikósok* (CHEE-kohsh-ohk), or Hungarian cowboys, are world famous for raising and training horses.

Climate

Like most countries in Central Europe, Hungary has a temperate climate. Its somewhat dry winters are cool, with temperatures that range from -4° to 0° Celsius.

Summers are comfortably warm and have a temperature range of 18° to 23° C. The climate does not vary much from region to region.

Below: At times, Hungary can have unusually cold winters, and temperatures have dropped as low as -34° C.

Plants and Animals

Only about 18 per cent of Hungary's land still has forests. The rest is either pasture land or has been cleared for farming. Forests are mainly beech, oak, lime and other **deciduous** trees.

The wildlife of Hungary's forests includes deer, wild pigs, foxes and rodents, and Hortobágy National Park has some of the largest birds in Europe. Aggtelek National Park has Ural owls and other birds rarely seen in Hungary.

Above: Many of the beech forests in Hungary are being cut down for use in industries.

Below: Storks (*below*), as well as cranes, ducks and herons, are among Hungary's native birds.

History

Until the end of the fourth century, the area that is now Hungary was part of the Roman Empire. Over the next four centuries, it was taken over by, first, Germanic tribes, then Slavs, and, later, the **nomadic** Avars. Around 800, after Charlemagne had defeated the Avars, Hungary became part of Europe's Carolingian empire.

In 892, the Carolingian emperor, Arnulf, asked the Magyars to help him defend his empire. Instead, the

Above: The Magyars are believed to have come to Hungary from southwestern Russia, near the Ural Mountains.

Left: The Museum of Aquincum, in Budapest, over-looks the ruins of the ancient Roman city of Aquincum.

Magyars, led by Árpád, fought against Arnulf and, by 907, had conquered the land known as Hungary. Árpád's great-great-grandson, Stephen I, became the first king of Hungary in 1000.

Mongols and Turks

In 1241, Hungary was **invaded** by the Mongols. Although they ruled for only one year, they killed about half of the people and badly damaged the country. When the Ottoman Turks invaded, in the 1500s, they divided the country into three regions, each with its own ruler.

The Hapsburg Years

When the Turks were driven out of Hungary in 1686, Austria's Hapsburg Empire took power. Rebellions in 1703 and 1848, however, brought reforms that restored a Hungarian **monarchy**. Although Hungary resisted Austria's attempts to take back full control of the country, a dual Austro-Hungarian monarchy was established in 1867. This government gave Hungary full independence, except in matters of defence, finance and foreign affairs.

Above: This castle in Fertőd belonged to the Esterházy family. This family gained its wealth and power by supporting the Hapsburg rulers.

Left: Emperor Charles I (1887–1922) was the last Hapsburg ruler of Austria.

World Wars

During World War I (1914–1918), Hungarians fought alongside the Germans. After the war, the Austro-Hungarian monarchy ended, and more than half of Hungary's land was given to neighbouring countries.

Although Hungarians wanted to be **neutral** in World War II, the Germans forced them to fight against the Allies and Hungary lost more land.

Communism

In November 1945, several seats in Hungary's first free elections were won by **communists**. With support from the former Soviet Union, Hungary soon became a one-party, communist state. Disliking communism, Hungarians revolted in 1956, but Soviet troops brutally crushed the uprising. Hungary remained a communist state until 1989.

Left:
To symbolise the end of communism in 1989, soldiers cut the barbed wire that had defined Hungary's borders.

King Matthias Corvinus (1443–1490)

Matthias I was a kind ruler and a good soldier. He defended Hungary against the Turks and made the country a European centre of art, culture and politics.

King Matthias Corvinus

Empress Maria Theresa (1717–1780)

As her father, Hapsburg king Charles III, had no male successors, Maria Theresa became Hungary's first female ruler in 1740.

Empress Maria Theresa

Lajos Kossuth (1802–1894)

After the 1848 rebellion, Lajos Kossuth quickly drew up the April Laws, greatly reducing Hapsburg control in Hungary. Kossuth fled the country in 1849, but the April Laws became the foundation of the Austro-Hungarian monarchy.

Lajos Kossuth

Government and the Economy

A **parliament** known as the National Assembly, or Országgyülés, is the main unit of government in Hungary. It has 386 members, who are elected by the people. All Hungarians over the age of 18 may vote. Members of the parliament elect Hungary's president, and the leader of the party that has the most members is the prime minister.

Above: Hungary's large and luxurious parliament building has 29 staircases.

Left: The building that houses Hungary's Országgyülés is in Budapest. It is the largest parliament building in Europe.

Local Government

At a local level, Hungary's government consists of 19 county councils in **rural** areas, 20 municipal county councils in **urban** areas, as well as the Metropolitan Council of Budapest, which serves the country's capital city. All of these councils are divided into smaller councils. Local governments in Hungary are responsible for health, education and transportation matters.

Above: Until June 2004, every Hungarian male above the age of 18 had to serve about a year of military service.

Economy

After the fall of communism in 1989, Hungary developed a **free-market economy**. The government encourages the growth of private businesses and tries to provide benefits for small- and medium-sized companies.

Above: The villagers of Tokaj grow a special type of grape used to make a popular wine called Aszú.

Only about 5 per cent of Hungary's economy is involved in agriculture. The country's farmers grow a variety of fruits and vegetables, including wheat, corn, rice, apples and plums.

Left: In addition to growing fruits and vegetables, Hungarian farmers raise cattle and many types of poultry, such as geese.

Natural Resources

Mining and metals have been important industries for Hungary's economy since the communist years. The country has large amounts of mercury, uranium, lead, **dolomite** and **bauxite**.

Above: This coal mine and the town around it are reminders of how important the mining industry was to Hungary's economy in the communist years.

Manufacturing

Most of the products Hungary **exports** are manufactured. They include paper, cars, construction materials, medicines and processed foods. About 30 per cent of the country's workforce have jobs in manufacturing.

People and Lifestyle

Nearly 90 per cent of Hungary's ten million people are descendants of the Magyars. The rest are Romanies, or Gypsies, and Germans, with small numbers of Serbs, Romanians and Slovaks. Over the course of Hungary's turbulent history, about five million Hungarians have **migrated** to other countries, including the United States.

Below: Families in Hungary are smaller today than before World War I. Most young Hungarians are choosing to have fewer children than their parents or grandparents had.

Left: Although thought of as wanderers, most of Hungary's Romanies have permanent homes in villages or near cities. This colourful culture is known all over the world, yet Romanies often face discrimination, especially related to education and employment.

Minority Groups

At about 4 per cent of the population, Romanies are the largest minority group in Hungary. About 3 per cent of Hungarians are Germans, the second largest minority. To protect minority groups, the government does not allow **discrimination** of any kind, and many of Hungary's laws specifically protect Romanies. Unfortunately, these laws are not always followed.

Family Values

Although Hungary's history of war and communism has broken down its traditional structure of large, close-knit families, Hungarians still try to bring many family members together on special occasions, such as Christmas and Easter and even family vacations. Modern Hungarian families usually include just a father, a mother and their unmarried children.

Above: Despite decades of communist interference in their religious heritage, most Hungarians still have a church ceremony when they get married.

Women in Hungary

Traditionally, men were the heads of Hungarian households. They worked on farms or in factories, while women stayed at home in their traditional roles as mothers and homemakers.

Since 1989, many Hungarian women have joined the country's workforce. With eight hours a day on the job, plus another four hours of household chores, they now have far less leisure time.

Below:
Today, many Hungarian women, especially those living in the cities, are financially independent.

Education

Hungary offers free education, and all children between the ages of six and sixteen must attend school. Elementary school lasts eight years. At age 15, most students start secondary, or high, school, which lasts four years. For their secondary education, students can choose to attend a college preparatory school, a technical school or a school specialising in music or fine arts.

Below: Hungarian parents usually enrol their children who are less than six years old in kindergartens.

Hungarian students begin higher education in colleges or universities at age 19. Not only is higher education free, but some students also receive an allowance to attend. Hungary has 80 schools of higher education. Nineteen are universities. The most respected universities are in Budapest. They include Budapest University of Economic Sciences and Eötvös Loránd University of Sciences.

Religion

Historically, the Roman Catholic Church has played a leading role in Hungarian society and politics. For many years, however, the country's communist government discouraged the practice of religion, often marching outside churches to disturb services. Today, Hungary has religious freedom, and the Roman Catholic Church is still an important part of Hungarian life.

Above: The artistic detail of Eger Cathedral's interior design is a breathtakingly beautiful sight.

Almost 70 per cent of Hungarians are Roman Catholics, 20 per cent are Calvinist Protestants, and 5 per cent are members of the Lutheran faith. The rest belong to minority religions such as Judaism.

Jews have lived in Hungary since the time of the Roman Empire, but after World War II and the **Holocaust**, their numbers dropped dramatically.

Below: The Dohány Street Synagogue, in Budapest, is the largest synagogue in Europe and the second largest in the world. Today, Hungary has about 60,000 Jews.

Language

Experts believe that the Hungarian language is one of a group of languages spoken mainly in northeastern Europe and western Siberia. It is very different from other European languages, but has borrowed some words from the Slavic, Latin, German and Turkish languages. Unique sounds in, for example, words such as *szálloda* (SAH-low-daw) and *rendörség* (REN-duhr-shage), which mean "hotel" and "police", are usually not recognisable to English speakers.

Left: A variety of newspapers and magazines are sold at news-stands on Hungary's streets.

Literature

Early Hungarian writings were mainly
religious works translated from Latin,
but non-religious literature flourished
in the 1700s. Famous writers at that
time included Benedek Komjáti, Gábor
Pesti and János Sylvester. Productivity
slowed down in the 1800s and 1900s
as the Turkish invasion, the Hapsburgs,
World Wars, German occupation and
communism smothered the creativity
of Hungarian writers.

Arts

Music

Hungary is the homeland of many well-known composers of classical music. *Hungarian Rhapsody No. 2*, composed by Franz Liszt (1811–1886), is still heard today. Piano pieces written by composer Béla Bartók (1881–1945) captured and preserved the folk music of Hungary and neighbouring countries.

Below: The state opera house in Budapest is Hungary's most luxurious venue for classical music concerts. A lavish ball also takes place at the opera house every year.

Left: To promote the Csárdás, the Hungarian Gypsy Company has been performing all over the world since about 1971.

Dance

When the Magyars settled in Hungary, they brought their dances with them. Considered **pagan** customs, these ancient dances were banned by the Roman Catholic Church in the tenth century. Since that time, Hungarian dance has been influenced by the music and steps of Italian, German and Romany dances. The *Csárdás* (CHAHR-dahsh), Hungary's national dance, was developed in the 1800s.

Embroidery

Hungarian **embroidery**, which is done by men as well as women, is a very artistic craft. Designs are mainly small to medium flower patterns in bright colours, usually stitched onto soft fabric, such as linen or cotton. The embroidery is then used to make a variety of items ranging from dresses to bedsheets and tablecloths. Hungarian tailors embroider directly onto coats, vests and cloaks and take pride in their intricate designs. Embroidery designs in Hungary vary from region to region.

Left: Traditional Hungarian lace and embroidery have been combined to create this colourful and decorative tablecloth.

Architecture

Budapest has been rebuilt so many times that its architecture reflects the city's history. Today, modern glass and metal structures stand side by side with historical buildings and even ancient ruins. Budapest also has some uniquely Hungarian architecture. Known as Hungarian art nouveau, it blends local folk art with Oriental designs.

Above:
The architecture of the Gresham Palast, a building located near the Chain Bridge in Budapest, is Hungarian art nouveau, a style that developed in the early 1900s.

Leisure

Most Hungarians like to spend their leisure time with family and friends. In the cities, couples often go out together to see a film or to have dinner at a restaurant. Some of the wealthier city residents own country homes, where friends and family members are invited to spend weekends and holidays.

Left: These older Hungarians are enjoying two favourite activities at the same time, playing chess and soaking in spas or hot springs.

Living in a landlocked country, Hungarians appreciate any chance to be in, on or near water. Lake Balaton, Hungary's largest single body of water, attracts thousands of local visitors and tourists every year. Activities on the lake include swimming, fishing and sailing. In the area around the lake, visitors can hike, camp or visit a zoo!

Above: Beautiful Lake Balaton is 97 km southwest of Budapest.

Sport

Over the years, Hungarians have won many Olympic gold medals. Swimmer Attila Czene won a gold medal in 1996. He also set an Olympic record for the 200-metre men's individual **medley**. At the 2004 Olympics, Hungary won eight gold medals in canoeing, shooting, fencing, wrestling, athletics, water polo and modern pentathlon; six silver medals and three bronze medals.

Above:
Hungarians are enthusiastic football fans. The stadiums are filled whenever home teams, such as Ferencváros and Kispest-Honvéd, are playing.

Hungary's national football team is known as the "Golden Team". In the 1950s, led by **legendary** football star Ferenc Puskás, the team was unbeaten for 30 games. Hungary also won the Olympic gold medal in 1952 and was the first European team to beat England at Wembley Stadium in London.

In recent years, tennis has become very popular in Hungary, especially with the younger and wealthier fans. Both Monica Seles and Martina Hingis are international tennis stars who have Hungarian roots.

Left: In 1998, tennis star Monica Seles was victorious over Alexandra Fusai of France in the All-England Championships at Wimbledon.

Holidays

Many of the holidays celebrated in Hungary are religious holidays, reflecting the strong position of the Roman Catholic faith in Hungarian life. St. Stephen's Day, on 20 August, honours King Stephen I of Árpád, who converted Hungarians to Christianity. The Roman Catholic Church declared Stephen a saint in 1083. Good Friday is another important religious holiday.

Below: Dancing is included in the public celebrations on St. Stephen's Day in the town of Eger.

Christmas is a particularly special holiday in Hungary. Preparations begin on St. Nick's Day (6 December). The night before, children place their shoes near a window, and St. Nick, who is Hungary's Santa Claus, fills clean shoes with candy and dirty shoes with twigs and stones. Christmas Eve starts with a feast. Then children stay out of sight while their parents decorate the Christmas tree. After opening gifts, the family attends a midnight Mass.

Food

Hungarians have a proud tradition of making hearty meals out of simple foods and inexpensive meats. Goulash is the best known Hungarian dish. It was originally the food of herdsmen on the Hungarian plains. Traditional goulash contained small pieces of meat mixed with onions and seasoned with **paprika**. Today, it includes vegetables such as carrots and potatoes.

Below: Paprika and garlic are so commonly used in Hungarian dishes that some shops in Hungary sell only these two items.

Left: Over the years, goulash ingredients have changed many times and have included many kinds of meats, spices and vegetables.

Breakfast in Hungary is a simple meal of fresh bread and a hot drink. Lunch usually starts with a clear soup. One popular soup is made of tomatoes and fish. A typical dinner will include spicy sausages, cheese and bread.

Hungarians like to end their meals with desserts. Dobos torte is a famous Hungarian dessert created in 1885 by a pastry chef named József Dobos. It is six thin layers of sponge cake with creamy **mocha** filling and topped with a caramel glaze.

Below: After the Turks introduced coffee to Hungary in the sixteenth century, coffeehouses spread rapidly. Traditional coffeehouses were very large and had elegant interiors.

	A	B	C	D
1				

CZECH REPUBLIC

SLOVAKIA

Carpathian

Aggtelek National Park

Danube

AUSTRIA

Northern Mountains
Mount Kékes
(1,014m) ▲

Eger

Fertõd

BUDAPEST
■ BUDAPEST

LITTLE ALFÖLD

Tisza

N

Bakony Mountains

GREAT ALFÖLD

Danube

Lake Balaton

SLOVENIA

CROATIA

SERBIA

Danube

HUNGARY

Legend

▬▬	International Boundary
───	County Boundary
■	Capital
●	City
～	River

E   F

M o u n t a i n s

UKRAINE

•Tokaj

Hortobágy
National Park

ROMANIA

Aggtelek National
    Park D2
Austria B2–A4

Bakony Mountains
    B3–C3
Budapest (city) C3
Budapest
    (county) C3

Carpathian
    Mountains
    B1–F1
Croatia A4–C5
Czech Republic
    A1–C1

Danube River
    A2–D5

Eger D2

Fertõd B3

Great Alföld D3–D4

Hortobágy National
    Park E3

Lake Balaton
    B4–C3
Little Alföld B3–C3

Mount Kékes D2

Northern
    Mountains D2

Romania E3–F5

Serbia C4–E5
Slovakia B2–F1
Slovenia A3–A5

Tisza River D5–F2
Tokaj E2

Ukraine F1–F2

Quick Facts

Official Name   Republic of Hungary

Capital   Budapest

Official Language   Hungarian

Population   10,074,000 (February 2006 estimate)

Land Area   93,030 square kilometres

Highest Point   Mount Kékes (1,014 metres)

Border Countries   Austria, Croatia, Romania, Serbia, Slovakia, Slovenia, Ukraine

Major Rivers   Danube, Tisza

Major Religions   Roman Catholic, Calvinist Protestant, Lutheran

Holidays   National Day (15 March)

Good Friday (March/April)

Saint Stephen's Day (20 August)

Saint Nick's Day (6 December)

Christmas Day (25 December)

Currency   Hungarian Forint (HUF 264 = Euro 1 as at May 2006)

Opposite: A colourful, patterned roof is a distinctive feature of Matthias Church in Budapest.

45

Glossary

arc: a curved line.

bauxite: the mineral from which aluminium is made.

communists: people who support a political system in which the government owns and controls all goods and resources.

deciduous: losing or shedding leaves each year.

discrimination: the practice of treating a person or group unfairly because of differences such as race or religion.

dolomite: a mineral that is the main source of magnesium in Earth's crust.

embroidery: the art of decorating fabric by hand-stitching colourful designs on it with a needle and thread.

exports (v): sells to other countries.

free-market economy: a system of producing and trading goods with little government control and prices that are normally determined by supply and demand.

Holocaust: the mass killing of European Jews by Nazis during World War II.

invaded: entered by force, usually by an enemy seeking to conquer or control.

landlocked: surrounded entirely by land.

legendary: historically famous for having outstanding abilities.

medley: a relay race in swimming in which each team member uses a different stroke.

migrated: moved permanently.

mocha: a chocolaty coffee flavour.

monarchy: a system of government controlled by a king or a queen.

neutral: not supporting either side in a dispute such as a war.

nomadic: moving from place to place with no permanent home.

pagan: based on material and physical pleasure without any religious or moral foundation.

paprika: a red cooking spice made of dried, finely ground sweet peppers.

parliament: a unit of government that makes laws.

plateaus: wide areas of high, flat land.

rural: related to the countryside.

tribes: distinct groups or divisions of people belonging to the same family, nation or race.

urban: related to cities and large towns.

More Books to Read

Hungarian Folk Tales. Myths and Legends series. Val Biro (Oxford University
  Press)
Causes and Consequences. World War One series. Simon Adams (Franklin Watts)

Websites

http://culture.gotohungary.co.uk/culture

www.castles.org/castles/Europe/Central_Europe/Hungary

www.fsz.bme.hu/hungary/budapest/kepek/szines.htm

www.zuzu.org/hung.html

Due to the dynamic nature of the Internet, some websites stay current longer than
others. To find additional websites, use a reliable search engine with one or more of
the following keywords to help you locate information about Hungary. Keywords:
Budapest, Csárdás, Danube, Eger, goulash, Hapsburg, Lake Balaton, Magyars.

Note to parents and teachers

Every effort has been made by the Publishers to ensure that these websites are
suitable for children, that they are of the highest educational value, and that they
contain no inappropriate or offensive material. However, because of the nature of
the Internet, it is impossible to guarantee that the contents of these sites will not be
altered. We strongly advise that Internet access is supervised by a responsible adult.

Index